WRESTLING SUPERSTARS

# ROMAN REIGNS

BY KAITLYN DULING

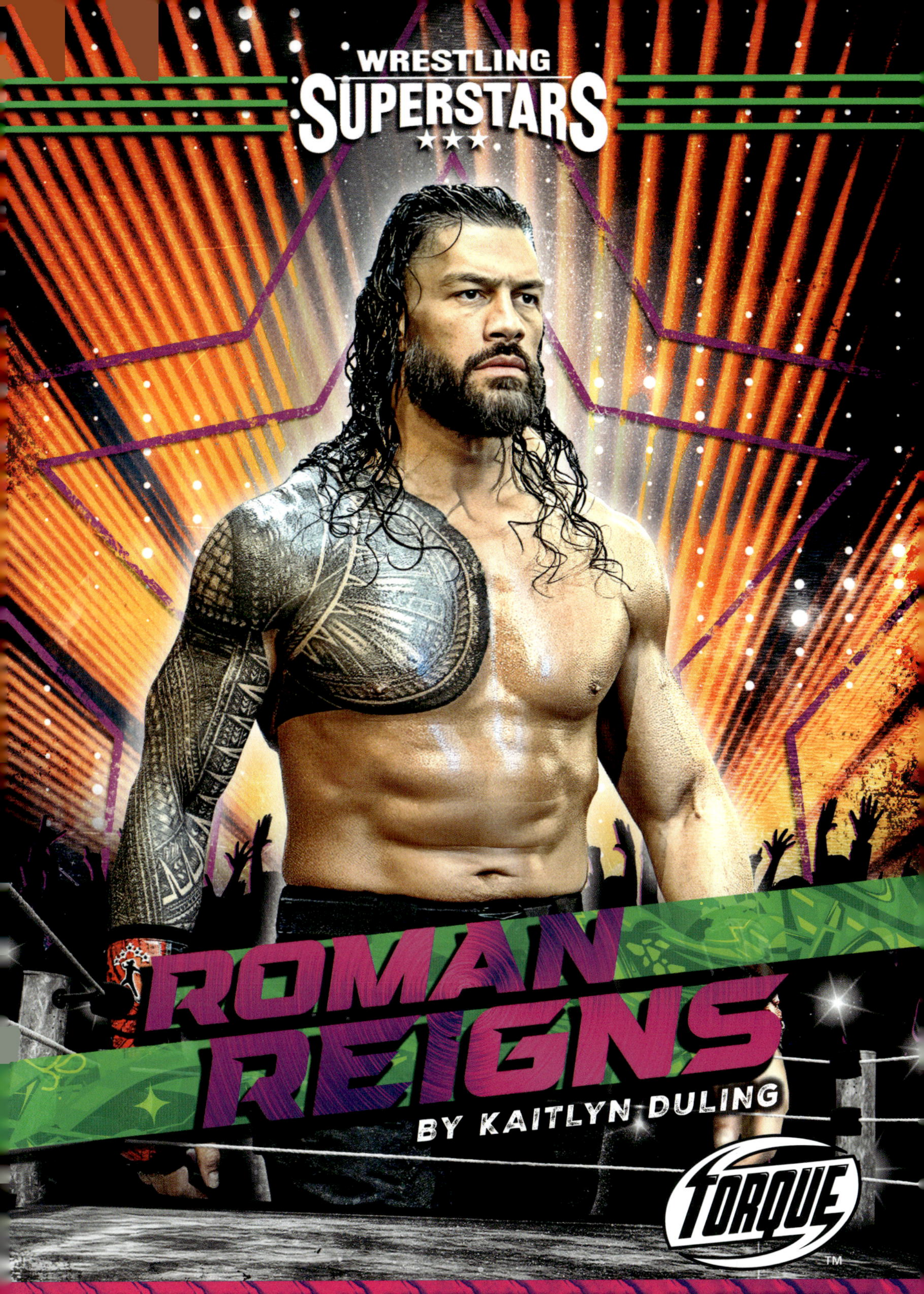

TORQUE

TORQUE, AN IMPRINT OF BELLWETHER MEDIA BY FLUTTERBEE

**Torque** brims with excitement perfect for thrill-seekers of all kinds. Discover daring survival skills, explore uncharted worlds, and marvel at mighty engines and extreme sports. In *Torque* books, anything can happen. Are you ready?

This edition first published in 2027 by Bellwether Media, Inc.



For information regarding permission, write to Bellwether Media, Inc., Attention: Permissions Department, 3500 American Blvd W, Suite 150, Bloomington, MN 55431.

Library of Congress Cataloging-in-Publication Data is available at www.loc.gov or upon request from the publisher.

ISBN: 9798898801113 (hardcover)
ISBN: 9798898802356 (ebook)

Editor: Suzane Nguyen Series Designer: Gabriel Hilger

Printed in the United States of America, North Mankato, MN.

# TABLE OF CONTENTS

# REIGNING CHAMPION

It has been a fierce **match** at WrestleMania 39. Roman Reigns and Cody Rhodes are battling for the **championship**. Rhodes flips Reigns onto the mat. He pins Reigns. Rhodes has almost won. Suddenly, Reigns breaks free!

Reigns attacks Rhodes with his top move, the Spear. The crowd roars. Reigns is the Undisputed WWE Universal Champion!

# WHO IS ROMAN REIGNS?

## LONGEST REIGN

Reigns held the WWE Universal Championship title for 1,316 days.

Roman Reigns is one of the biggest stars in **World Wrestling Entertainment (WWE)**. He held the WWE Universal Championship **title** longer than any other wrestler.

# ROMAN REIGNS

**BIRTHDAY**
MAY 25, 1985

**HOMETOWN**
PENSACOLA, FLORIDA

**COMPANY**
WWE

**HEIGHT**
6'3"

**THEME SONG**

"I Am Greatness"
def rebel

WWE MUSIC

Despite Reigns being a **heel**, fans love him. His most recent nickname is the Tribal Chief. He is the leader of a famous wrestling **faction**, the Bloodline.

# A WRESTLING FAMILY

REIGNS WITH DWAYNE "THE ROCK" JOHNSON

Reigns was born into a family of wrestlers. His dad, uncle, cousins, and brother were WWE wrestlers. His family is connected to Dwayne "The Rock" Johnson!

As a child, Reigns liked to play football. He dreamed of being a football player. In high school, he played football for two schools.

### ALL IN THE FAMILY

Reigns's cousins, The Usos, are famous WWE tag team wrestlers.

In college, Reigns played football for four years. After college, Reigns played **professional** football. He signed with the Minnesota Vikings and the Jacksonville Jaguars.

In 2008, Reigns signed to play football for a Canadian football team. Reigns played for one season. That same year, he **retired** from football.

REIGNS PLAYING COLLEGE FOOTBALL

## WRESTLING CANCER

During a health checkup with the Minnesota Vikings, Reigns found out he had cancer. In 2008, he was well enough to play football again.

# FAVORITES

**SPORT**
FOOTBALL

**NFL TEAM**
SAN FRANCISCO 49ERS

**SNEAKER**
AIR JORDANS

**HOBBY**
VIDEO GAMES

# GOOD GUY GONE BAD

## TIMELINE

**2010**

Reigns signs with WWE

**2014**

Reigns wins Superstar of the Year at the Slammy Awards

In 2010, Reigns signed his first WWE **contract**. He started with a **developmental ring** in Florida. Reigns practiced his skills with Florida Championship Wrestling.

That same year, Reigns made his TV **debut**. Early on, he was a **face**. His first ring name was Leakee. Later, he started using the name Roman Reigns.

**2015**

Reigns becomes a WWE Champion

**2018**

Reigns takes a break from WWE when his cancer returns

**2020**

Reigns returns to WWE as a heel

In 2012, Reigns joined a faction called The Shield. Reigns and his teammates Dean Ambrose and Seth Rollins won many matches together. During his time with The Shield, Reigns won his first **Slammy Award**.

In 2014, The Shield ended. Reigns was on his own. His hard work paid off. That year, he won Superstar of the Year at the Slammy Awards.

## WRESTLER OF MANY NAMES

Reigns has many nicknames, including The Big Dog and The Head of the Table.

Reigns became a WWE Champion in 2015. WWE wanted him to be their biggest star. Some were unhappy with this. But Reigns gained many new fans.

In 2018, Reigns's cancer returned. He took a break from wrestling. Reigns made a **comeback** in 2019. Then he took another break. Fans thought he retired from wrestling!

# TITLES
as of 2026

2x UNDISPUTED WWE CHAMPION (FORMERLY CALLED WWE UNIVERSAL CHAMPION)

4x WWE WORLD CHAMPION

1 WWE GRAND SLAM CHAMPION

7x SLAMMY AWARD WINNER

2x WWE ROYAL RUMBLE WINNER

Reigns returned as a heel during the 2020 SummerSlam. His fans loved it! He also returned with a new nickname, the Tribal Chief.

From 2020 to 2024, Reigns was the WWE Universal Champion. He held this title for four years. He lost the title to Cody Rhodes at WrestleMania 40. After losing, Reigns turned face again.

# TOP MOVES

## THE SUPERMAN PUNCH

POUNDS FIST INTO THE MAT BEFORE LEAPING AND PUNCHING THE OPPONENT IN THE FACE

## THE SPEAR

RUNS INTO THE OPPONENT, THEN TACKLES THEM TO THE MAT

## THE SAMOAN DROP

CARRIES OPPONENT ON HIS SHOULDERS, THEN FALLS BACKWARDS SO THE OPPONENT CRASHES INTO THE MAT

# REIGNS RETURNS

Aside from wrestling, Reigns is also an actor. He has acted in several movies, including the 2026 movie, *Street Fighter*. Reigns has even voiced characters in shows and movies! He hopes to take on more acting roles.

CAST OF THE 2026 MOVIE, *STREET FIGHTER*

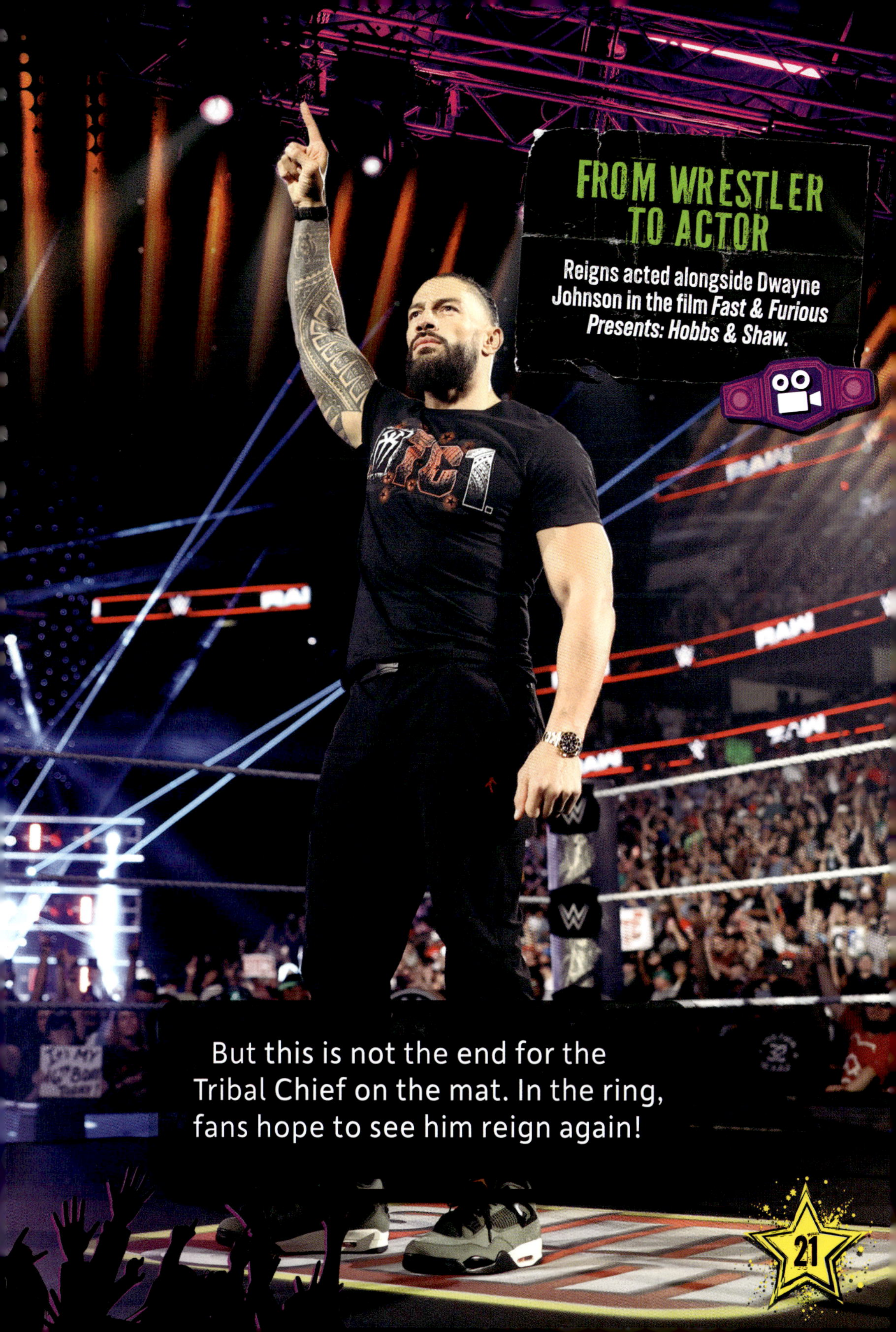

## FROM WRESTLER TO ACTOR

Reigns acted alongside Dwayne Johnson in the film *Fast & Furious Presents: Hobbs & Shaw.*

But this is not the end for the Tribal Chief on the mat. In the ring, fans hope to see him reign again!

# GLOSSARY

**championship**—a contest to decide the best team or person

**comeback**—a return

**contract**—an official agreement

**debut**—a person's first appearance or performance

**developmental ring**—a place where new wrestlers can practice their skills before moving to a larger stage

**face**—a hero character

**faction**—a group of wrestlers who band together

**heel**—a villain character

**match**—a contest between two wrestlers

**professional**—related to a person or athlete who makes money wrestling

**retired**—stopped working

**Slammy Award**—an award given to celebrate the best moments, matches, and wrestlers of WWE

**title**—the status of being the champion

**World Wrestling Entertainment (WWE)**—the world's largest professional wrestling and sports entertainment company

# TO LEARN MORE

## AT THE LIBRARY


Arnez, Lynda. *Be a Pro Wrestler.* Buffalo, N.Y.: Gareth Stevens Publishing, 2024.

Monnig, Alex. *Roman Reigns.* Minneapolis, Minn.: Abdo, 2024.

Smith, Elliott. *Steve Austin vs. Dwayne Johnson.* North Mankato, Minn.: Capstone Press, 2025.


## ON THE WEB

**FACTSURFER**

Factsurfer.com gives you a safe, fun way to find more information.

1. Go to www.factsurfer.com
2. Enter "Roman Reigns" into the search box and click 🔍.
3. Select your book cover to see a list of related content.

# INDEX



The images in this book are reproduced through the courtesy of: Diego Serrano/ Wikimedia Commons, front cover; WWE/ Contributor/ Getty Images, pp. 3, 6, 7, 8, 9, 11 (Roman Reigns), 18, 19 (all), 21, 22; Ronald Martinez/ Staff/ Getty Images, pp. 4, 5 (all); Mike Zarrilli/ Stringer/ Getty Images, p. 10; BillionPhotos.com, p. 11 (football); San Francisco 49ers/ Wikimedia Commons, p. 11 (San Francisco 49ers logo); xMarshall, p. 11 (air jordans); Lansk, p. 11 (video games); WENN Rights Ltd/ Alamy Stock Photo, pp. 12, 14 (bottom); CHANDAN KHANNA/ Stringer/ Getty Images, p. 13 (2015); Zuma Press, Inc./ Alamy Stock Photo, p. 14 (top); Jed Jacobsohn/ Contributor/ Getty Images, p. 15; Ron Elkman/ Sports Imagery/ Contributor/ Getty Images, p. 16; Rob Tringali/ Contributor/ Getty Images, p. 17; Frank Micelotta/ Contributor/ Getty Images, p. 20.